Fabian Anya

Unveiling Catholic Program for You

Fabian Anya

Unveiling Catholic Program for You

Blessed Hope Publishing

Imprint

Any brand names and product names mentioned in this book are subject to trademark, brand or patent protection and are trademarks or registered trademarks of their respective holders. The use of brand names, product names, common names, trade names, product descriptions etc. even without a particular marking in this work is in no way to be construed to mean that such names may be regarded as unrestricted in respect of trademark and brand protection legislation and could thus be used by anyone.

Cover image: www.ingimage.com

Publisher:
Blessed Hope Publishing
is a trademark of
Dodo Books Indian Ocean Ltd. and OmniScriptum S.R.L publishing group

120 High Road, East Finchley, London, N2 9ED, United Kingdom
Str. Armeneasca 28/1, office 1, Chisinau MD-2012, Republic of Moldova, Europe
Printed at: see last page
ISBN: 978-620-4-18816-4

Unveiling Catholic Program for You

Fabian Anya

+2348160766584

fabianokechukwu91@gmail.com

Scriptural References Are Taken from King James Version.

Appreciation

I want to appreciate all lovers of truth. I also appreciate everyone that looks beyond this present life and is mindful of where to spend eternity.

Preface

Many have been sent to hell fire by Catholic Church. With smiles, cheerful face and offer of false hope, Catholic Church have pushed her adherents into the burning pit of hell to regret forever. Much more saddening is the fact, that the heirs of salvation are also seduced to worship idols. They obey Catholic Church in observance of their idolatrous festivals, because

their leaders are not discerning enough to unveil the subtilty of this Mystery Babylon.
Pentecostal and Protestant church leaders are preoccupied with amassing wealth, they give more
attention to Mechanical miracles and fake signs and wonders that will multiply their
followership and wealth, and pay less attention to studying the scriptures to feed their followers
with knowledge that will make them wise and help them decode deception and stay saved. The
end is near, please change!

"Turn, O backsliding children, saith the LORD; for I am married unto you: and I will take you
one of a city, and two of a family, and I will bring you to Zion: And I will give you pastors
according to mine heart, which shall feed you with knowledge and understanding." **Jerremiah
3 verses 14 to 15**

The Church leaders, instead of restoring the backsliding Christians, justify their sins, and tell
them it doesn't matter, that God is so merciful that He will not punish sinners. The law of truth
is no longer in their mouth, instead, they replace equity with iniquity.

True servants of God should declare truth, equity and peace. They should expose and destroy
falsehood, instead of being part of deception, this is what the Bible says:

"The law of truth was in his mouth, and iniquity was not found in his lips: he walked with me
in peace and equity, and did turn many away from iniquity.
For the priest's lips should keep knowledge, and they should seek the law at his mouth: for he *is*
the messenger of the LORD of hosts. But ye are departed out of the way; ye have caused many
to stumble at the law; ye have corrupted the covenant of Levi, saith the LORD of
hosts. Therefore have I also made you contemptible and base before all the people, according as
ye have not kept my ways, but have been partial in the law." **Malachi 2 verses 6 to 9**
Saints of God are the kings of the earth, who drink her cup of fornication. see

"And hast made us unto our God kings and priests: and we shall reign on the earth."
Revelation 5 verse 10

These kings of the earth are made to commit idolatry by their leaders who obey Catholic doctrines and festivals that contradict the Bible. These leaven of the Catholic, which sends even the saints to hell, is unveiled in this book, to educate the Christian masses to stay away from the damnation which results from the deception.

Table of Contents

Chapter One

Diversion of Salvation

Jesus Christ came to seek and to save the lost. He instituted the process through which to accomplish the salvation of humanity. The laid down rule is found in the Bible;

"And he said unto them, Go ye into all the world, and preach the gospel to every creature.

He that believeth and is baptized shall be saved; but he that believeth not shall be damned."

Mark 16 verses 15 to 16

It is very clear that Jesus Christ laid down two requirements for the salvation of Man.

1. Believe
2. Be baptized.

He that does not believe shall be damned.

Only persons with the ability to reason can believe or disbelieve, so this requirement is expected from matured persons. People with the ability to think for themselves, and take binding decisions are the only ones qualified and required to fulfill the number one condition which is Believe. Infants lack the ability to think, reason and take binding decisions. So, infants are not the people that Jesus Christ want to be baptized. Infants are already justified by the Lord Jesus Christ. So, they are not yet lost. In fact, the Lord said that the Kingdom of God is for them.

"But Jesus said, Suffer little children, and forbid them not, to come unto me: for of such is the kingdom of heaven." Mathew 19 verse 14

Infant Baptism and the consequences

Infant baptism confuses the victims when they grow up to age of reasoning to believe that they are already baptized. So, they continue in that illusion. This disqualifies them from salvation. It is important to note that these victims of infant baptism were not emersed in water as the Lord Jesus Christ set the example. Catholic Church merely sprinkles water upon their head. This is a mockery of what Jesus Christ did. It is not baptism. Infants lack ability to believe and to confess that Jesus Christ is the Son of God. Those whose head were sprinkled with water in infant should submit themselves for baptism when they become adults with ability to believe and confess that Jesus Christ is the Son of God, otherwise, they will be lost in hell fire.

"Then cometh Jesus from Galilee to Jordan unto John, to be baptized of him. But John

forbad him, saying, I have need to be baptized of thee, and comest thou to me? And Jesus answering said unto him, Suffer it to be so now: for thus it becometh us to fulfil all righteousness. Then he suffered him. And Jesus, when he was baptized, went up straightway out of the water: and, lo, the heavens were opened unto him, and he saw the Spirit of God descending like a dove, and lighting upon him: And lo a voice from heaven, saying, This is my beloved Son, in whom I am well pleased." Mathew 3 verses 13 to 17

Jesus Christ was baptized In River Jordan. His Father was pleased with this action of Christ, and declared: "This is my beloved Son, in whom I am well pleased."

Jesus Christ equally declared that Baptism is fulfilment of the righteousness.

Therefore, anyone that skips it, has not fulfilled righteousness.

"And Philip said, If thou believest with all thine heart, thou mayest. And he answered and said, I believe that Jesus Christ is the Son of God. And he commanded the chariot to stand still: and they went down both into the water, both Philip and the eunuch; and he baptized him. And when they were come up out of the water, the Spirit of the Lord caught away Philip, that the eunuch saw him no more: and he went on his way rejoicing. The Eunuch believed and confessed with his mouth that Jesus Christ is the Son of God. He and Philip went down into the water, and he was baptized. Baptism also is for the remission of sin. Those that are not baptized properly, retain their sins, this will damn them in hell fire." Acts 8 verses 37 to 39

"Then Peter said unto them, Repent, and be baptized every one of you in the name of Jesus Christ for the remission of sins, and ye shall receive the gift of the Holy Ghost." Act 2:38

Emersion baptism signifies that we are buried with Christ in Baptism and will resurrect with Him. So, those that are not emersed in water, are denied the opportunity to be buried with

Christ and to resurrect with Him. Catholics that have water sprinkled on their head in infant lack the opportunity to resurrect with Christ, as they are not buried with Him.

"Buried with him in baptism, wherein also ye are risen with *him* through the faith of the operation of God, who hath raised him from the dead." **Colossians 2 verse 12**

Baptism makes believers one with Christ, and unifies believers of all races into one body of Christ. So, those that are not baptized are not one with Christ, neither are they part of the body of Christ. This is how the Catholics are not one with Christ, and are not part of the body of Christ.

"For as many of you as have been baptized into Christ have put on Christ. There is neither Jew nor Greek, there is neither bond nor free, there is neither male nor female: for ye are all one in Christ Jesus." Galatians 3 verse 27 to 28

"There is one body, and one Spirit, even as ye are called in one hope of your calling; One Lord, one faith, one baptism, One God and Father of all, who is above all, and through all, and in you all." Ephesians 4 verses 4 to 6

Catholics should awake to the fact that they are on their way to hell. They should also realize that they are responsible for what happens to their soul, and leave that idolatrous institution when they still have the time.

Chapter Two

Cup of Fornication

When the people of God worship other gods, it is spiritual fornication or adultery against the Lord. When Samaria and Jerusalem worshipped idols, God called them adulterous wives. He called them twin sisters - Aholah and Aholibah. The church is bride of Christ. Any church that commits idolatry is deemed to commit fornication or adultery against the Lord. Such church denomination is damned.

"And they committed whoredoms in Egypt; they committed whoredoms in their youth: there were their breasts pressed, and there they bruised the teats of their virginity. And the names of them were Aholah the elder, and Aholibah her sister: and they were mine, and they bare sons and daughters. Thus were their names; Samaria is Aholah, and Jerusalem Aholibah. And Aholah played the harlot when she was mine; and she doted on her lovers, on the Assyrians her neighbours, Which were clothed with blue, captains and rulers, all of them desirable young men, horsemen riding upon horses. Thus she committed her whoredoms with them, with all them that were the chosen men of Assyria, and with all on whom she doted: with all their idols she defiled herself. Neither left she her whoredoms brought from Egypt: for in her youth they lay with her, and they bruised the breasts of her virginity, and poured their whoredom upon her. Wherefore I have delivered her into the hand of her lovers, into the hand of the Assyrians, upon whom she doted. These discovered her nakedness: they took her sons and her daughters, and slew her with the sword: and she became famous among women; for they had executed judgment upon her. And when her sister Aholibah saw this, she was more corrupt in her inordinate love than she, and in her whoredoms more than her sister in her whoredoms. She doted upon the Assyrians her neighbours, captains and rulers clothed most gorgeously, horsemen riding upon horses, all of them desirable young men. Then I saw that she was defiled, that they took both one way, And that she increased her whoredoms: for when she saw men pourtrayed upon the wall, the images of the

Chaldeans pourtrayed with vermilion, Girded with girdles upon their loins, exceeding in dyed attire upon their heads, all of them princes to look to, after the manner of the Babylonians of Chaldea, the land of their nativity: And as soon as she saw them with her eyes, she doted upon them, and sent messengers unto them into Chaldea. And the Babylonians came to her into the bed of love, and they defiled her with their whoredom, and she was polluted with them, and her mind was alienated from them. So she discovered her whoredoms, and discovered her nakedness: then my mind was alienated from her, like as my mind was alienated from her sister. Yet she multiplied her whoredoms, in calling to remembrance the days of her youth, wherein she had played the harlot in the land of Egypt. For she doted upon their paramours, whose flesh is as the flesh of asses, and whose issue is like the issue of horses. thus thou calledst to remembrance the lewdness of thy youth, in bruising thy teats by the Egyptians for the paps of thy youth. Therefore, O Aholibah, thus saith the Lord GOD; Behold, I will raise up thy lovers against thee, from whom thy mind is alienated, and I will bring them against thee on every side; The Babylonians, and all the Chaldeans, Pekod, and Shoa, and Koa, and all the Assyrians with them: all of them desirable young men, captains and rulers, great lords and renowned, all of them riding upon horses. And they shall come against thee with chariots, wagons, and wheels, and with an assembly of people, which shall set against thee buckler and shield and helmet round about: and I will set judgment before them, and they shall judge thee according to their judgments. And I will set my jealousy against thee, and they shall deal furiously with thee: they shall take away thy nose and thine ears; and thy remnant shall fall by the sword: they shall take thy sons and thy daughters; and thy residue shall be devoured by the fire. They shall also strip thee out of thy clothes, and take away thy fair jewels. Thus will I make thy lewdness to cease from thee, and thy whoredom brought from the land of Egypt: so that thou shalt not lift up thine eyes unto them, nor remember Egypt any more. For thus saith the Lord GOD; Behold, I will deliver thee into the hand of them whom thou hatest, into the hand of them from whom thy mind is alienated: And they shall deal with thee hatefully, and shall take away all thy labour, and shall leave thee naked and bare: and the nakedness of thy whoredoms shall be discovered, both thy lewdness and thy whoredoms. I will do these things unto thee, because thou hast gone a whoring after the heathen, and because thou art polluted with their idols. Thou hast walked in the way of thy sister; therefore will I give her cup into thine hand. Thus saith the Lord GOD; Thou shalt drink of thy sister's cup deep and large: thou shalt be laughed to scorn and had in derision; it containeth much. Thou shalt be filled with drunkenness and sorrow, with the cup of astonishment and desolation, with the cup of thy sister Samaria. Thou shalt even drink it and suck it out, and thou shalt break the sherds thereof, and pluck off thine own breasts: for I have spoken it, saith the Lord GOD. Therefore thus saith the Lord GOD; Because thou hast forgotten me, and cast me behind thy back, therefore bear thou also thy lewdness and thy whoredoms. The LORD said moreover unto me; Son of man, wilt thou judge Aholah and Aholibah? yea, declare unto them their abominations; That they have committed adultery, and blood is in their hands, and with their idols have they committed adultery, and have also caused their sons, whom they bare unto me, to pass for them through the fire, to devour them." Ezekiel 23 verse 3 to 37

"Wives, submit yourselves unto your own husbands, as unto the Lord. For the husband is the head of the wife, even as Christ is the head of the church: and he is the saviour of the body. Therefore as the church is subject unto Christ, so let the wives be to their own husbands in everything." Ephesians 5 verses 22 to 24

The Church is to be subject to Christ. This means that the primary role of the church is to obey Christ! God values obedience more than sacrifice. A church that is not submissive to Christ, seizes to be his bride.

"If ye keep my commandments, ye shall abide in my love; even as I have kept my Father's commandments, and abide in his love." Joh 15:10

The Bible says that who you obey is your Lord. Therefore, a church that obeys Satan has made Satan her lord. Obedience to the word of God is what makes any church the bride of Christ.

God hates rebellion. Satan rebelled against Him in heaven, He cast him out of His presence in spite of all the precious metals He used to create him and the wisdom and talents he bestowed on him.

God punishes everyone that rebels against His word. Hananiah the Prophet, made people of Israel to trust in a lie, and rebel against the true word of God, which Jeremiah, the Prophet preached to them. So, God destroyed him. All that will make people to believe in a lie in this generation, will also be thrown to hell fire.

"Then said the prophet Jeremiah unto Hananiah the prophet, Hear now, Hananiah; The LORD hath not sent thee; but thou makest this people to trust in a lie. Therefore thus saith the LORD; Behold, I will cast thee from off the face of the earth: this year thou shalt die, because thou hast taught rebellion against the LORD. So Hananiah the prophet died the same year in the seventh month." Jeremiah 28 verses 15 to 17

"An evil man seeketh only rebellion: therefore a cruel messenger shall be sent against him." Pro 17:11

The Lord warned us in the Bible that nobody should add to his word or remove anything from it.

"Ye shall not add unto the word which I command you, neither shall ye diminish ought from it, that ye may keep the commandments of the LORD your God which I command you." Deuteronomy 4:2

Pagan practices and festivals were brought into the church, and rationalized as worthy of practice, though the Bible did not recommend them. This is rebellion against the word of Christ. He commanded the church to not add anything to his words or remove anything from it.

"I Jesus have sent mine angel to testify unto you these things in the churches. I am the root and the offspring of David, and the bright and morning star. And the Spirit and the bride say, Come. And let him that heareth say, Come. And let him that is athirst come. And whosoever will, let him take the water of life freely. For I testify unto every man that heareth the words of the prophecy of this book, If any man shall add unto these things, God shall add unto him the plagues that are written in this book: And if any man shall take away from the words of the book of this prophecy, God shall take away his part out of the book of life, and out of the holy city, and from the things which are written in this book." Revelation 22 verses 16 to 19

Catholic Church rebelled against this commandment of the Lord, and seduced other Churches to also rebel against the Lord by practicing things that Jesus Christ never commanded them to practice.

Catholic church worships the goddess of fertility and spring - Esostrae, disguising her as Easter.

Esostrae

The word Easter is derived from the word Esostrae or Esostrae, the Anglo-Saxon goddess of spring and fertility. The council of Nicaea in 325 A.D, ordered that Easter should be observed on the first Sunday following the first full moon after the spring Equinox (March 21). Easter, therefore can fall on any Sunday between March 22 and April 25. Equinox is either of the two moments in the year when the sun is exactly above the equator, and day and night are equal length, also either of the two points in the sky where the ecliptic (the sun's annual pathway) and the celestial equator intersect. The vernal equinox marking the beginning of spring in the northern hemisphere, occurs about March 2, when the sun moves north across the celestial equator.

The autumnal equinox falls about September 23, as the sun cross the celestial equator going south.

Easter is a pagan festival that has been on before the birth of Christ. Pagan Roman Empire celebrates this festival in honor of the goddess of spring and fertility. In the early years of Christianity, King Herod persecuted the Church and killed Apostle James the brother of John, sons of Zebedee. He also arrested Peter to be murdered after Easter celebration. The pagan Roman Empire and their Emperors honored Easter and didn't want to desecrate this their holy day with the murder of the "heretic" Apostle Peter, so he confined him in the prison awaiting to be murdered after their Easter festival.

"Now about that time Herod the king stretched forth his hands to vex certain of the church. And he killed James the brother of John with the sword. And because he saw it pleased the Jews, he proceeded further to take Peter also. (Then were the days of unleavened bread.) And when he had apprehended him, he put him in prison, and delivered him to four quaternions of soldiers to keep him; intending after Easter to bring him forth to the people."
Act 12 verses 1 to 4

Obviously, if Easter was a Christian Festival, King Herod would neither honor it nor celebrate it.

Easter is idolatrous festival which Catholic Church introduced into the church in 325 A.D at the council of Nicaea. Unfortunately, her prostitute daughters – the evangelical, Pentecostal and other churches joined her in this annual global idolatry.

By keeping Sunday Protestants submit to the Vatican's authority over them,

Pentecostal and Protestant Churches submit themselves under the authority of the Pope and his Cardinals by worshipping the goddess of fertility and spring – Esostrae – as Easter. Vatican, astrologically fixes the date for Easter celebration, and the Pentecostal, evangelical and spiritual churches that claim to be protestants obey the Pope and participate in this idolatry, which the Bible condemns as observance of time:

"Ye shall not eat anything with the blood: neither shall ye use enchantment, nor observe times." Lev 19:26

"When thou art come into the land which the LORD thy God giveth thee, thou shalt not learn to do after the abominations of those nations. There shall not be found among you any one that maketh his son or his daughter to pass through the fire, or that useth divination, or an observer of times, or an enchanter, or a witch, Or a charmer, or a consulter with familiar spirits, or a wizard, or a necromancer. For all that do these things are an abomination unto the LORD: and because of these abominations the LORD thy God doth drive them out from before thee." Deu 18 verses 9 to 12

It takes astrology (observation of time) to determine when Spring Equinox will be, when the next full moon will be and the next Sunday following the full moon after spring equinox. This is condemned by Jehovah as idolatry. This is what Catholic Church does through her leaders. They fix the time for Easter celebration, all her harlot daughters – the other church denominations concur, and still call themselves protestants. By this they worship goddess of spring and fertility, and still claims to be bride of Christ. This is why Jesus Christ said

"Strive to enter in at the strait gate: for many, I say unto you, will seek to enter in, and shall not be able. When once the master of the house is risen up, and hath shut to the door, and ye begin to stand without, and to knock at the door, saying, Lord, Lord, open unto us; and he shall answer and say unto you, I know you not whence ye are: Then shall ye begin to say, We have eaten and drunk in thy presence, and thou hast taught in our streets. But he shall say, I

Mother of Lies

Catholic Church also worships Mithra the infant god of stone in the guise of celebrating the birth of Jesus Christ. They seduced unsuspecting and ignorant Church denominations and Christians world-wide to do same.

To further confuse Christians to believe in her lies, Catholic Church fabricated a lie that Jesus Christ was crucified on Good Friday, and that He resurrected on Sunday. They hope, by this lie, to convince Christians to believe in Easter celebration, as celebration of the resurrection of Christ, and also worship on Sunday as the day Jesus Christ resurrected. All these are lies!

Now the true information provided in the Bible is as follows;

Jesus Christ told us that he would stay three days and three nights in the grave before resurrecting.

"For as Jonas was three days and three nights in the whale's belly; so, shall the Son of man be three days and three nights in the heart of the earth." Mathew 12 verse 40

Referring to what Catholic Church taught the Christian world, if Christ was crucified on Good Friday;

The day time of Friday was the first **day,**

The Night time of Friday was the first **Night.**

The day time of Saturday was the second **day,**

The night time of Saturday was the second **night.**

Jesus Christ resurrected before Sunday morning because Mary Magdaline went to the grave early Sunday Morning, while it was yet dark, but Christ wasn't in the grave.

"The first day of the week cometh Mary Magdalene early, when it was yet dark, unto the sepulcher, and seeth the stone taken away from the sepulcher. Then she runneth, and cometh to Simon Peter, and to the other disciple, whom Jesus loved, and saith unto them, They have taken away the Lord out of the sepulcher, and we know not where they have laid him. Peter therefore went forth, and that other disciple, and came to the sepulcher.So they ran both together: and the other disciple did outrun Peter, and came first to the sepulchre" John 20 verses 1 to 4

If, the teachings of Catholic Church that Christ was crucified on Good Friday is true, it then means that Jesus Christ spent only two days and two nights in the grave. Christ told us in Mathew 12:40 that he would spend three days and three nights in the grave. So, Catholic Church lied to the entire world on this issue.

"When Jesus had spoken these words, he went forth with his disciples over the brook Cedron, where was a garden, into the which he entered, and his disciples. And Judas also, which betrayed him, knew the place: for Jesus oft times resorted thither with his disciples. Judas then, having received a band of men and officers from the chief priests and Pharisees, cometh thither with lanterns and torches and weapons. Jesus therefore, knowing all things that should come upon him, went forth, and said unto them, Whom seek ye? They answered him, Jesus of Nazareth. Jesus saith unto them, I am he. And Judas also, which betrayed him, stood with them. And Simon Peter followed Jesus, and so did another disciple: that disciple was known unto the high priest, and went in with Jesus into the palace of the high priest. But Peter stood at the door without. Then went out that other disciple, which was known unto the high priest, and spake unto her that kept the door, and brought in Peter. Then saith the damsel that kept the door unto Peter, Art not thou also one of this man's disciples? He saith, I am not. And the servants and officers stood there, who had made a fire of coals; for it was cold: and they warmed themselves: and Peter stood with them, and warmed himself.

The High Priest Questions Jesus

The high priest then asked Jesus of his disciples, and of his doctrine. Jesus answered him, I spake openly to the world; I ever taught in the synagogue, and in the temple, whither the Jews always resort; and in secret have I said nothing. Why askest thou me? ask them which heard me, what I have said unto them: behold, they know what I said. And when he had thus spoken, one of the officers which stood by struck Jesus with the palm of his hand, saying, Answerest thou the high priest so? Jesus answered him, If I have spoken evil, bear witness of the evil: but if well, why smitest thou me? Now Annas had sent him bound unto Caiaphas the high priest.

Peter Denies Jesus Again

And Simon Peter stood and warmed himself. They said therefore unto him, Art not thou also one of his disciples? He denied it, and said, I am not. One of the servants of the high priest, being his kinsman whose ear Peter cut off, saith, Did not I see thee in the garden with him? Peter then denied again: and immediately the cock crew." John 18 verses 1 to 27

"The first day of the week cometh Mary Magdalene early, when it was yet dark, unto the sepulchre, and seeth the stone taken away from the sepulchre." John 20 verse 1

This means Jesus Christ resurrected before Sunday morning, He didn't spend the day time of Sunday in the grave, and neither did He spend the night time of Sunday in the grave. This means that He spent only two days and two nights in the grave according to Catholic teaching; This does not agree with what the Lord Jesus Christ told the church in Mathew 12:40 that He will spend three days and three nights in the grave. So, these Church leaders have lied and deceived the churches they are leading. Of course, the objectives of these lies are two;

    1.To seduce Christians to worship sun god on Sunday.

    2.To seduce Christians to celebrate and worship goddess of spring and fertility (Esostrae) on Easter, which they falsely claimed to be the celebration of the resurrection of Christ.

Churches that celebrate Easter are idol worshippers. No idol worshiper goes to heaven after death. Sunday worship is permissive, and not perfect will of God for the Church.

Now the true information provided in the Bible is as follows;

Jesus Christ was arrested in the night, and taken to the palace of the High Priest, with Peter following the mob a far off. Before the cock crew two times in the morning Peter has denied Him three times. In the morning being Thursday, day of preparation for the Sabbath, the High Priest, along with the mob, escorted Christ to the Judgment Hall to be judged by Pilate, but the High Priest didn't enter the judgment hall so that he would not be defiled as he was to sanctify himself to be ready to sacrifice the pass over (Pascal) lamb by 3 pm that Thursday. Jesus Christ was condemned and crucified at midday, the exact hour for slaughtering the Pascal Lamb.

He was also buried same Thursday so that He would not remain on the cross the next day Friday being preparation day for Saturday Sabbath.

So, the day time of Thursday was the **first day**,

The night time of Thursday was the **first night.**

The day time of Friday was the **second day,**

The Night time of Friday was the **second Night.**

The day time of Saturday was the **third day,**

The night time of Saturday was the **third night.**

Jesus Christ resurrected at the last hour of Saturday night that completed his stay in the grave three days and three nights. This agrees with His words in Mathew 12:40

"For as Jonas was three days and three nights in the whale's belly; so shall the Son of man be three days and three nights in the heart of the earth." Mat 12:40

The shift of worship day from Saturday to Sunday, and celebration of Easter as memorial of the resurrection of Christ is a calculation by Satan through Catholic Church to seduce Christians to worship idol.

Christmas

Christmas was first celebrated by Roman Catholic Church on 25th December 336AD. Early Christians did not celebrate Christmas. The Catholic Encyclopedia says: "Early Christians did not observe birthdays, not even Christ birth; The Catholic theologian Origen a.d. 185 – 232 acknowledged that in the scripture, sinners alone, not saints celebrated birthday. The Bible did not institute Christmas. It has nothing to do with Christ. Christmas trees and decorations, giving of gifts, Santa clause decorations and burbles are not biblical traditions. It is wrong and sinful to adopt pagan traditions to be used to worship Christ.

Jesus Christ did not command His disciples to celebrate his birth day. Neither did he command them to celebrate his resurrection. Throughout His stay on the earth, He didn't celebrate His birth day once. His Apostles didn't celebrate it either, and didn't command anybody to do so. No king of Israel celebrated birth day in the Bible. Birthday celebration is alien to the Jews. The Kings that celebrated their birthdays in the Bible were all gentile sinner kings. King Pharaoh of Egypt celebrated his birthday and beheaded his Botler during the celebration. King Herod of Roman Empire celebrated his birthday and beheaded John the Baptist during the celebration. This celebration seemingly connotes evil! Today, church leaders even celebrate their birth day. I think Christians are Christlike people! Who do Bishops and Pastors of our time emulate by celebrating birthdays? Is it Christ, his Apostles or Pharaoh and Herod? Indeed, hell is enlarging herself with these compromisers.

Mithra

Pagan Rome celebrated the birthday of Mithra, the god of the unconquerable sun in December 25. They believe that Mithra the infant god was born of a rock. This pagan idolatrous tradition was adopted by Roman Catholic Church and renamed Christmas.

Christmas tree

Also, the demon known as Brumalia was celebrated as god of the sun by Pagan Rome after the winter solstice. The symbol was a little green tree which is supposed to have grown over night out of a dead wood. Today it is called Christmas tree.

"For they also built them high places, and images, and groves, on every high hill, and under every green tree." 1st Kings 14 verse 23

All this evil in the name of Christmas was introduced into the Church to provoke Jehovah to anger and jealousy.

Catholic church told all these lies to seduce unsuspecting seekers of Christ to worship idols and be sent to hell fire. Hello, beloved Christian, if you are celebrating Easter and Christmas, be sure Catholic Church has roped you in for damnation of hell fire. Flee the wrath of God to come.

"And there shall in no wise enter into it anything that defileth, neither whatsoever worketh abomination, or maketh a lie: but they which are written in the Lamb's book of life." Revelation 21 verse 27

"Ye shall not add unto the word which I command you, neither shall ye diminish ought from it, that ye may keep the commandments of the LORD your God which I command you." Deuteronomy 4 verse 2

Catholic Church rebelled against the commands of Jesus Christ, which says nobody should add or remove from His Words. They add anything they chose to add and rationalize it. They also remove whatever they want to remove. They equally change the laws of God and His chosen day of worship, claiming that they are above the Bible. They changed the law of Sabbath and seduced Christians to start worshipping on Sunday.

Jehovah charged His people to keep Sabbath. He further warned them not to forget Sabbath.

"Keep the sabbath day to sanctify it, as the LORD thy God hath commanded thee."
Deuteronomy 5 verse 12

Neither Jesus Christ nor His apostles adopted Sunday worship. The Apostles worshipped on Saturday. This is why they did not collect food supplies on Saturday, rather they did that on Sunday.   This should not be interpreted by anybody to mean that the apostles shifted day of worship to Sunday.

"Now concerning the collection for the saints, as I have given order to the churches of Galatia, even so do ye. 1Co 16:2 Upon the first day of the week let every one of you lay by him in store, as God hath prospered him, that there be no gatherings when I come." 1st Corinthians 16 verse 1

Jesus Christ spent forty days with His disciples after resurrection before He ascended to heaven. He did not tell His disciples to shift day of worship to Sunday.

It was Pagan Roman Emperors that made laws commanding all their subjects to worship their sun god on the venerable day of the Sun. The year 321 AD Emperor Constantine made the first Sunday law and Christians were forced to join in the worship of sun god.

"Let all the judges and town people and the occupation of all trades rest on the venerable day of the sun" Edict of March, 7, 321 AD.

Catholic records affirmed that they are the ones that caused the shift from Saturday Sabbath to Sunday, and that it is the mark of their authority over the Bible.

"Sunday is the mark of our authority. The church is above the Bible, and his transference of Sabbath observance is a proof of that fact." The Catholic Record of London, Ontario, Sept. 1 1923.

That Christians are at liberty to worship God any day of their choice, is permissive will of God. God is seeking those that will prove His perfect will and obey it.

They rebel against God by changing the day he wants to be worshipped (Saturday), to commemorate that He is the Creator of the Universe to Sunday, the venerable day of the sun god.

This is why the bible calls all the churches that obey Catholic Church prostitute daughters of the Great Whore. They drink of her cup of abomination and will suffer the same plague with her, unless they repent.

Reverend Fathers

The Church has only one father. This father is in heaven. He is God Almighty and no one else. He is jealous of this title, and warned the Church to not call anyone else her father on the earth.

"For unto us a child is born, unto us a son is given: and the government shall be upon his shoulder: and his name shall be called Wonderful, Counsellor, The mighty God, The everlasting Father, The Prince of Peace. "Isaiah 9 verse 6

Forever and ever, Jesus Christ remains the father of the Church, the everlasting father of the church. He does not retire from this title, neither does he delegate it to anyone. Instead, he warned the Church to not call anyone her father upon the earth.

"And call no *man* your father upon the earth: for one is your Father, which is in heaven."
Mathew 23 verse 9

Catholic Church defied that command, and choose to call and address their clergy as Reverend Fathers. It is blasphemous for anyone to arrogate the Title of God to himself.

Catholic also extends this blasphemy to her aging ignorant members by ordaining them Good Mothers and Good Fathers. However, they monetized these titles, as they make their wealthy aging members pay much money to purchase it. Meanwhile, Jesus Christ said, no one is good, except the Father who is in heaven. This title is to ensure that they actually offend God more and get to hell.

"And, behold, one came and said unto him, Good Master, what good thing shall I do, that I may have eternal life? And he said unto him, Why callest thou me good? there is none good but one, that is, God: but if thou wilt enter into life, keep the commandments." Mathew 19 verse 16

"He sent redemption unto his people: he hath commanded his covenant forever: holy and reverend is his name." Psalm 111 verse 9

The name of Jehovah is reverend. No other name merits to be addressed as reverend. The Pentecostal and evangelical churches have also erred in this, just for vain glory.

Image Worship

God warned His people to not make image of anything, and to not bow before them.

"Thou shalt have no other gods before me. Thou shalt not make unto thee any graven image, or any likeness of anything that is in heaven above, or that is in the earth beneath, or

that is in the water under the earth: Thou shalt not bow down thyself to them, nor serve them: for I the LORD thy God am a jealous God, visiting the iniquity of the fathers upon the children unto the third and fourth generation of them that hate me;" Exodus 20 verses 3 to 5

Catholic Church introduced images in the church. They mold images within and outside of their cathedrals, they bow before statues of different kinds. To extend image worship to other church denominations, Pope Alexandar VI forced the image of his son Caesarea Borgia on the church as the image of Christ. Today many ignorant Christians honor the image of Caesarea Borgia as the image of Christ. Many church denominations hang this image on their walls. Some of them draw it on their church sign posts. Some Christians hang this image in their homes. Thus, they become guilty of idolatry. God warned Christians against making images. There is no time he allowed Himself to be carved or molded by anyone. Christians that use images of anything to represent Christ are guilty of idolatry. They don't care about the word of God which says; "Thou shalt not make unto thee any graven image, or any likeness *of anything* that *is* in heaven above, or that *is* in the earth beneath, or that *is* in the water under the earth:" This shows they don't reverence God. They may claim ignorant, this alibi will not save them from eternal hell. They are commanded to study the Bible:

"This book of the law shall not depart out of thy mouth; but thou shalt meditate therein day and night, that thou mayest observe to do according to all that is written therein: for then thou shalt make thy way prosperous, and then thou shalt have good success" Joshua 1 verse 8

Ignorance of the Bible is not an excuse, repent.

"And if a soul sin, and commit any of these things which are forbidden to be done by the commandments of the LORD; though he wist it not, yet is he guilty, and shall bear his iniquity." Leviticus 5 verse 17

"My people are destroyed for lack of knowledge: because thou hast rejected knowledge, I

*will also reject thee, that thou shalt be no priest to me: seeing thou hast forgotten the law of
thy God, I will also forget thy children." Hosea 4 verse 6*

Wedding Rings

Wedding rings used in churches today, is idolatrous. It's not encouraged anywhere in the Bible.
It is imported from Pagan Egypt Idolatry. The Pharaohs used Rings to represent their sun god,
since ring is round like the sun. They also believe that rings represent eternity, as it has no
beginning and ending. The tradition of exchanging wedding rings began with ancient pagan
Rome and Greece in about second century. Prostitute church adopted it from these pagans in
about 9th century. Unfortunately, this has become a very effective tool in the hands of Satan to
fill hell fire with the soul of Christians.

Idolatrous Nature of Rings and Ornaments

*"And God said unto Jacob, Arise, go up to Bethel, and dwell there: and make there an altar
unto God, that appeared unto thee when thou fleddest from the face of Esau thy
brother. Then Jacob said unto his household, and to all that were with him, Put away the
strange gods that are among you, and be clean, and change your garments: And let us arise,
and go up to Bethel; and I will make there an altar unto God, who answered me in the day of
my distress, and was with me in the way which I went. And they gave unto Jacob all the
strange gods which were in their hand, and all their earrings which were in their ears; and
Jacob hid them under the oak which was by Shechem." Genesis 35 verses 1 to 4*

Note that the wives of Jacob were coming from idolatrous community as at the time Jacob
asked them to remove the idols in their midst. He didn't specifically ask them to remove the
earrings, but they removed that also as idol. Why? They knew it was treated as idol where they
were coming from, that's why they removed the earrings with them as idols.

Though God allowed Children of Israel to ask Egyptians of these ornaments, it never – the -
less became a snare to Israel in the wilderness. This made God to order them to strip
themselves of the ornaments if He would continue to lead them on the way.

*"And when the people saw that Moses delayed to come down out of the mount, the people
gathered themselves together unto Aaron, and said unto him, Up, make us gods, which shall
go before us; for as for this Moses, the man that brought us up out of the land of Egypt, we
wot not what is become of him. And Aaron said unto them, Break off the golden earrings,
which are in the ears of your wives, of your sons, and of your daughters, and bring them unto
me. And all the people brake off the golden earrings which were in their ears, and brought
them unto Aaron. And he received them at their hand, and fashioned it with a graving tool,
after he had made it a molten calf: and they said, These be thy gods, O Israel, which brought
thee up out of the land of Egypt. And when Aaron saw it, he built an altar before it; and
Aaron made proclamation, and said, Tomorrow is a feast to the LORD. And they rose up
early on the morrow, and offered burnt offerings, and brought peace offerings; and the
people sat down to eat and to drink, and rose up to play. And the LORD said unto Moses, Go,
get thee down; for thy people, which thou broughtest out of the land of Egypt, have corrupted
themselves: They have turned aside quickly out of the way which I commanded them: they
have made them a molten calf, and have worshipped it, and have sacrificed thereunto, and
said, These be thy gods, O Israel, which have brought thee up out of the land of Egypt. And
the LORD said unto Moses, I have seen this people, and, behold, it is a stiffnecked
people: Now therefore let me alone, that my wrath may wax hot against them, and that I may
consume them: and I will make of thee a great nation." Exodus 32 verses 1 to 10*

God would have destroyed all of them, if not for the intervention of Moses. Ornaments and
rings always rear up their head as idol, and is a provocation to the Almighty God. When God
forgave them, He didn't want to lead them anymore. Moses begged God to continue leading
them. Then God gave a condition, under which He may consider to lead them. That condition is
that they should strip themselves of the ornaments on them.

"And I will send an angel before thee; and I will drive out the Canaanite, the Amorite, and the Hittite, and the Perizzite, the Hivite, and the Jebusite: Unto a land flowing with milk and honey: for I will not go up in the midst of thee; for thou art a stiffnecked people: lest I consume thee in the way. And when the people heard these evil tidings, they mourned: and no man did put on him his ornaments. For the LORD had said unto Moses, Say unto the children of Israel, Ye are a stiffnecked people: I will come up into the midst of thee in a moment, and consume thee: therefore now put off thy ornaments from thee, that I may know what to do unto thee. And the children of Israel stripped themselves of their ornaments by the mount Horeb." Exodus 33 verses 2 to 6

This means that, for a child of God to maintain the leading or guidance of God, he or she should strip himself or herself of ornaments!

Earrings and ornaments became a snare to Gideon and his household. After fighting and subduing the Midianites, he couldn't subdue the idolatrous power of earrings and ornaments.

"Then the men of Israel said unto Gideon, Rule thou over us, both thou, and thy son, and thy son's son also: for thou hast delivered us from the hand of Midian. And Gideon said unto them, I will not rule over you, neither shall my son rule over you: the LORD shall rule over you. And Gideon said unto them, I would desire a request of you, that ye would give me every man the earrings of his prey. (For they had golden earrings, because they were Ishmaelites.) And they answered, We will willingly give them. And they spread a garment, and did cast therein every man the earrings of his prey. And the weight of the golden earrings that he requested was a thousand and seven hundred shekels of gold; beside ornaments, and collars, and purple raiment that was on the kings of Midian, and beside the chains that were about their camels' necks. And Gideon made an ephod thereof, and put it in his city, even in Ophrah: and all Israel went thither a whoring after it: which thing became a snare unto Gideon, and to his house." Judges 8 verses 22 to 27

The labor of love which Gideon bestowed upon the people was forgotten quickly, and seventy of his sons were slain in a day because of the idol he molded with the earrings and ornaments.

"Neither shewed they kindness to the house of Jerubbaal, namely, Gideon, according to all the goodness which he had shewed unto Israel." Judges 8 verse 35

"And he went unto his father's house at Ophrah, and slew his brethren the sons of Jerubbaal, being threescore and ten persons, upon one stone: notwithstanding yet Jotham the youngest son of Jerubbaal was left; for he hid himself." Judges 9 verse 5

Christians are warned to not wear ornaments and earrings. It is idolatrous.

"In like manner also, that women adorn themselves in modest apparel, with shamefacedness and sobriety; not with broided hair, or gold, or pearls, or costly array; " 1st Timothy 2 verse 9

Unfortunately, demons behind these ornaments have blocked the ears and minds of multitudes of Christians and their leaders so much that they would rather burn in unquenchable fire of hell than give up earrings and ornaments. This is very sad. My beloved Christian, say no to jewels, ornaments, earrings, nose rings, ankle rings, necklaces and medals. These will land you in eternal hell and lake of fire!   Also read Isaiah 3:

"…walking and mincing as they go, and making a tinkling with their feet: Therefore the Lord will smite with a scab the crown of the head of the daughters of Zion, and the LORD will discover their secret parts. In that day the Lord will take away the bravery of their tinkling ornaments about their feet, and their cauls, and their round tires like the moon, The chains, and the bracelets, and the mufflers, The bonnets, and the ornaments of the legs, and

the headbands, and the tablets, and the earrings, The rings, and nose jewels, The changeable suits of apparel, and the mantles, and the wimples, and the crisping pins, The glasses, and the fine linen, and the hoods, and the vails." Isaiah 3 verses 16 to 23

Doctrine of Devils

"Now the Spirit speaketh expressly, that in the latter times some shall depart from the faith, giving heed to seducing spirits, and doctrines of devils; Speaking lies in hypocrisy; having their conscience seared with a hot iron; Forbidding to marry, and commanding to abstain from meats, which God hath created to be received with thanksgiving of them which believe and know the truth." 1st Timothy 4 verse 1 to 3

The Bible further warns Christians to beware of doctrines of devils which will be rampant in the later days. One of these doctrines of devils is Forbidding to marry and abstaining from eating meat.

Catholic Church forbids her clergy to marry, and commands Catholics to abstain from meat during Ash Wednesday. They are ruled by seducing spirits which speak lies in hypocrisy.

Almost all the Christian world is seduced by Catholic to celebrate Easter, Christmas and worship on Sundays, thus they are condemned for hell. Now the Pope is calling for law to force everyone to observe Sunday rest or be imprisoned or killed.

Remember, the Lord Jesus Christ said:

"Jesus answered, My kingdom is not of this world: if my kingdom were of this world, then would my servants fight, that I should not be delivered to the Jews: but now is my kingdom not from hence. " John 18 verse 36

The Kingdom of Christ is not of this world. So, the blue (Sunday) laws made by some governments of the world are spear headed by the Prince of this world. The same Prince seeks worship through Sunday observance.

"Hereafter I will not talk much with you: for the prince of this world cometh, and hath nothing in me." John 14 verse 30

Jesus Christ is the Lord of every genuine Christian. Our kingdom is not of this world. If you, as a Christian still obey the Prince of this world, worshipping idols in the disguise of Christmas or Easter, you are damned. Beware! Keep yourself pure!

Chapter Three

Mother of Harlots

"And there came one of the seven angels which had the seven vials, and talked with me, saying unto me, Come hither; I will shew unto thee the judgment of the great whore that sitteth upon many waters: With whom the kings of the earth have committed fornication, and the inhabitants of the earth have been made drunk with the wine of her fornication. So he carried me away in the spirit into the wilderness: and I saw a woman sit upon a scarlet coloured beast, full of names of blasphemy, having seven heads and ten horns. And the woman was arrayed in purple and scarlet colour, and decked with gold and precious stones and pearls, having a golden cup in her hand full of abominations and filthiness of her fornication: And upon her forehead was a name written, MYSTERY, BABYLON THE

GREAT, THE MOTHER OF HARLOTS AND ABOMINATIONS OF THE EARTH. And I saw the woman drunken with the blood of the saints, and with the blood of the martyrs of Jesus: and when I saw her, I wondered with great admiration." Revelation 17 verses 1 to 6

*"**And he saith unto me, The waters which thou sawest, where the whore sitteth, are peoples, and multitudes, and nations, and tongues." Revelation 17 verse 15***

Ignorant Pastors and Christians call Catholic Church Mother Church. Indeed, she is the mother of harlots. All the Churches that adopt her doctrines and idolatrous festivals are her harlot daughters. She sits on many waters. The waters represent peoples, multitudes, nations and tongues. Catholic Church is everywhere in the world. Her idolatrous festivals are observed in every nation and by every tongue. Christmas is observed every where in the world. Easter is observed everywhere in the world. Even Born- again Christians, ignorantly drink of her cup of fornication – Christmas and Easter. Thus, she makes Kings of the earth drink of her cup of fornication, and the inhabitants of the earth have been made drunk with the wine of her fornication.

She is full of the names of blasphemy. Reverend Father as a title for her clergy is blasphemous. VICARIOUS FILII DEI written on the tiara of the Pope, which means substitute for Christ is blasphemy, as none can be substituted for Christ. VICARIOUS FILII DEI in roman figure translates to 666.

Judgment of God on the Harlot Daughters of Catholic Church.

All Church denominations that obey Catholic Church, will also suffer the same damnation with her. Jesus Christ didn't command the Church to celebrate His Birthday. He didn't command the Church to celebrate his resurrection falsely named Easter by Catholic Church. Jesus Christ warned the Church to not add anything to His word, and to not remove anything from His word;

but Catholic church added Christmas and Easter, her harlot daughters obeyed her instead of Christ. The judgment of Christ on this harlot daughters of Catholic Church is recorded in:

"And unto the angel of the church in Thyatira write; These things saith the Son of God, who hath his eyes like unto a flame of fire, and his feet are like fine brass; I know thy works, and charity, and service, and faith, and thy patience, and thy works; and the last to be more than the first. Notwithstanding I have a few things against thee, because thou sufferest that woman Jezebel, which calleth herself a prophetess, to teach and to seduce my servants to commit fornication, and to eat things sacrificed unto idols. And I gave her space to repent of her fornication; and she repented not. Behold, I will cast her into a bed, and them that commit adultery with her into great tribulation, except they repent of their deeds. And I will kill her children with death;" Revelation 2 verses 18 to 23

Catholic Church compares with Prophetess Jezebel that seduced Christians to commit fornication and adultery with her. The Lord Jesus Christ said:

"I will kill her children with death;" unless they repent.

Christmas and Easter celebration has eaten deep into the fabrics of Churches, unless there is a turn-away from this sedition, almost all Christians are going to hell fire. Another destructive epidemic that is taking souls to hell in mass is jewel or ornaments. Many faithful Christians are ending up in hell because they refuse to acknowledge that earrings, wedding rings etc. are idolatry. This is the end time. Repent now, and escape the wrath of God.

Judgment of the great whore that sitteth upon many waters:

"And the ten horns which thou sawest upon the beast, these shall hate the whore, and shall make her desolate and naked, and shall eat her flesh, and burn her with fire. For God hath put in their hearts to fulfil his will, and to agree, and give their kingdom unto the beast, until

the words of God shall be fulfilled. And the woman which thou sawest is that great city, which reigneth over the kings of the earth." Revelation 17 verses 16 to 18

"And after these things I saw another angel come down from heaven, having great power; and the earth was lightened with his glory. And he cried mightily with a strong voice, saying, Babylon the great is fallen, is fallen, and is become the habitation of devils, and the hold of every foul spirit, and a cage of every unclean and hateful bird. For all nations have drunk of the wine of the wrath of her fornication, and the kings of the earth have committed fornication with her, and the merchants of the earth are waxed rich through the abundance of her delicacies. And I heard another voice from heaven, saying, Come out of her, my people, that ye be not partakers of her sins, and that ye receive not of her plagues. For her sins have reached unto heaven, and God hath remembered her iniquities. Reward her even as she rewarded you, and double unto her double according to her works: in the cup which she hath filled fill to her double. How much she hath glorified herself, and lived deliciously, so much torment and sorrow give her: for she saith in her heart, I sit a queen, and am no widow, and shall see no sorrow. Therefore shall her plagues come in one day, death, and mourning, and famine; and she shall be utterly burned with fire: for strong is the Lord God who judgeth her." Revelation 18 verses 1 to 8

Catholics and other Christians that are drinking her cup of fornication, the Lord is commanding you to come out of her or be destroyed along with her.

"And I heard another voice from heaven, saying, Come out of her, my people, that ye be not partakers of her sins, and that ye receive not of her plagues." Revelation 18 verse 4

If you remain in this false church, or continue to drink of her cup of fornication, it means that your name is not written in the Lamb's books of life from the foundation of the earth. So, your end will be eternal death in lake of fire!

"And all that dwell upon the earth shall worship him, whose names are not written in the

book of life of the Lamb slain from the foundation of the world." Revelation 13 verse 8

Chapter Four

Vampire Institution

"And there was given unto him a mouth speaking great things and blasphemies; and power was given unto him to continue forty and two months. And he opened his mouth in blasphemy against God, to blaspheme his name, and his tabernacle, and them that dwell in heaven. And it was given unto him to make war with the saints, and to overcome them: and power was given him over all kindreds, and tongues, and nations. And all that dwell upon the earth shall worship him, whose names are not written in the book of life of the Lamb slain from the foundation of the world. If any man have an ear, let him hear." Revelation 13 verses 5 to 9

Catholic Church was given power to rule the world for forty-two prophetic months, to blaspheme God and kill saints of Christ within that period of time. The forty - two prophetic months amounts to one thousand, two hundred and sixty years.

One prophetic month equals 30 days.

"And the waters prevailed upon the earth an hundred and fifty days." Genesis 7 verse 11

"Rain began on the 17th day of the 2nd Month. It rained for 150 days". Genesis. 7 verse 24.

It stopped raining on 17th day of 7th month. That is, it rained for five months. The five months equals 150 days. So one month = 30 days.

Therefore, 42 months reign of the beast in Rev. 13:5 and 11:2 is 42 x 30 = 1260 days.

1 prophetic day = 1 year.

"After the number of the years in which ye searched the land, even forty days, each day for a year…" Numbers 14 verse 34

"… I have appointed thee each day for a year". Ezekiel 4 verse 6

Therefore, 1260 days equals 1260 years. The scripture stated that the beast - 7th world ruler - will rule for 42 months (1260 prophetic days), which is 1260 years.

The Pope assumed power in 538 A.D, and was deposed in 1798 AD when emperor Napoleon of France conquered Papal Army and took him to France in exile. He died in 1799 in France while in exile.

1798 minus 538 = 1260 years. Thus, the Pope ruled for 1260 years (42 Prophetic months) to fulfill the prophecy.

Here is a brief excerpt from the history of fall of the 7th World Ruler

"The French Directory demanded that the Papacy revoke, retract, and disannul all bulls, briefs, rescripts, and decrees affecting ecclesiastical affairs in France issued since the beginning of the Revolution in 1787. This Pius VI refused, declaring he would oppose it with force, and broke off the parley. Napoleon took Imola, the Romagna, the duchy of Urbino, routed the papal army, and made new overtures to the pope."

PIUS VI DETHRONED ON ANNIVERSARY IN SISTINE CHAPEL

. — Meantime, on this very same day — February 15 — on the anniversary of his elevation to the pontificate, Pius VI repaired to the Sistine Chapel, and was receiving the felicitations of the Sacred College of cardinals, when, in the midst of the ceremony, shouts penetrated the conclave, intermingled with the strokes of axes on the doors. Soon General Haller, a Swiss Calvinist, with a band of his soldiers, broke into the chapel, and declared that the pope's reign was at an end.[22] (Painting appears on page 754.) His Swiss guards were dismissed, and republican soldiers substituted. Ferrara, Bologna, and Romagna (Peter's patrimony)

were taken over, and the cardinals were stripped of authority and possessions. Eight were arrested and sent to the Civita Castellana.[23] The glory, honor, and power had vanished. Soldiers were quartered in the papal palace. Such was the stroke of the sword at Rome. It was the end of an epoch in papal history long before predicted in the prophecies of Holy Writ. Trevor goes so far as to say:

"The territorial possessions of the clergy and monks were declared national property, and their former owners cast into prison. The papacy was extinct: not a vestige of its existence remained; and among all the Roman Catholic powers not a finger was stirred in its defence. The Eternal City had no longer prince or pontiff; its bishop was a dying captive in foreign lands; and the decree was already announced that no successor would be allowed in his place."

DIES AT VALENCE, FRANCE, IN 1799. — But the pope was still in the heart of Italy. So Pius VI was transferred to Florence, constantly under guard of French dragoons. Next his transfer to Parma was decided upon, the departure to take place at 2 A.M. As the pope was suffering from partial paralysis, his guards had great difficulty in effecting the transfer. From here he was taken to Turin, and finally to the French fortress at Valence, in Dauphiny arriving there July 14, 1799, broken with fatigue and sorrow. He died there on the 28th."

Thus, the scripture was fulfilled which says:

"He that leadeth into captivity shall go into captivity: he that killeth with the sword must be killed with the sword. Here is the patience and the faith of the saints." Revelation. 13 verse 10

The military conquest of the Pope and his loss of political sovereignty is the mortal wound which was inflicted on the beast.

"And I saw one of his heads as it were wounded to death; and his deadly wound was healed: and all the world wondered after the beast." Revelation.13 verse 3

Within this period of time, Catholic Church persecuted Born – again Christians as heretics, and killed millions of them through her doctrine of inquisition and various crusades. Careful and reputed historians of the Catholic Inquisition estimated that 50 million people were slaughtered for the crime of "heresy" by Roman Persecutors between 606 and the middle of 19th century. Many protestants, because of their fate were burnt at the stake.

William Tyndale was refused permission to translate the Bible into English Language by Catholic Bishop. He fled to Germany and printed his first New Testament, and smuggled them into England. His translation was banned and burned by Catholic Authorities.

Eventually, Tyndale was betrayed by Henry Philips to ducal authorities, representing the Holy Roman Empire. He was seized in Antwerp in 1535, and held in the castle of Vilvoorde (Fulford) near Brussels. He was strangled in October, 1536 and his body burned at the stake. Those that executed Tyndale were under orders from King Henry VIII, Sir Thomas Moore, and Bishop John Stokesley.

Jan Hus, a theologian, Preacher and Rector of Prague University, on the 6th of July, 1415 was burned at the stake at the council of Constance, for his views and criticism of Catholic Church.

Thus, Catholic Church fulfilled the prophecy of drinking the blood of the saints of God.

"And it was given unto him to make war with the saints, and to overcome them: and power was given him over all kindreds, and tongues, and nations. " Revelation 13 verse 7

Chapter five

Beastly Monarch

"As concerning the rest of the beasts, they had their dominion taken away: yet their lives were prolonged for a season and time." Daniel 7 verse 12

Seven global governments have ruled the world. The seventh one was Papacy. Prophecy of Daniel said their dominion was taken away, yet their lives were prolonged for a season and time.

This means that the nations that ruled the world globally, are not extinct. They are still in existence, only that their global political power was taken away. For example, Papacy was overthrown by Emperor Napoleon Bonaparte of France, but Papacy is not extinct, she is still in existence, and waxing strong.

"And there are seven kings: five are fallen, and one is, and the other is not yet come; and when he cometh, he must continue a short space. And the beast that was, and is not, even he is the eighth, and is of the seven, and goeth into perdition." Revelation 17 verses 10 to 11

"And he saith unto me, The waters which thou sawest, where the whore sitteth, are peoples, and multitudes, and nations, and tongues." Revelation 17 verse 15

"And the beast that was, and is not, even he is the eighth, and is of the seven, and goeth into perdition." Revelation 17 verse 11

The above verse is saying that the Beast (king) that was in global government before, but is not wielding political power now, ruled the seventh global government, and will rule in the 8th Global government.

The order of their global governance before was as follows:

1. Egypt
2. Asyria
3. Babylon
4. Medes and Persia
5. Greece under Alexandar the Great
6. Roman Empire
7. Holy Roman Empire under Papacy.

Papacy will rule again as the 8th and last gentile government. He will be overthrown by Christ through the war of Armageddon.

World War III, will prepare the ground for New World Order to finalize arrangements for global governance. The Bible said they will divide the world into ten geopolitical zones. They will appoint ten Kings to rule these zones, a king for a zone. These ten kings will later, unanimously hand over global power to the Pope. Thus, he will become the 8th global Monarch or Dictator.

"And the ten horns which thou sawest are ten kings, which have received no kingdom as yet; but receive power as kings one hour with the beast. These have one mind, and shall give their power and strength unto the beast." Revelation 17 verses 12 to 13

The Pope at this time is above Catholic Church and Holy See. There will be religious ecumenism. The religion this time, will not be Christianity or Catholicism. The Dictator will be worshipped as God. Anyone that does not receive the number of his name 666 as identity, and sign of loyalty will not be allowed to buy or sell, and will be tortured and killed

"And he causeth all, both small and great, rich and poor, free and bond, to receive a mark in their right hand, or in their foreheads: And that no man might buy or sell, save he that had the mark, or the name of the beast, or the number of his name. Here is wisdom. Let him that hath understanding count the number of the beast: for it is the number of a man; and his number is Six hundred threescore and six." Revelation 13 verses 16 to 18

At time, Vatican City will not be relevant, more so, it will be a threat to the new government and Religion. So, the new government will set it on fire, and destroy it completely.

"And the ten horns which thou sawest upon the beast, these shall hate the whore, and shall make her desolate and naked, and shall eat her flesh, and burn her with fire. For God hath put in their hearts to fulfil his will, and to agree, and give their kingdom unto the beast, until the words of God shall be fulfilled. And the woman which thou sawest is that great city, which reigneth over the kings of the earth." Revelation 17 verses 16 to 18

It is obvious that Vatican City is great, and reigns over the kings of the earth. It has great influence over United Nations and her input is always sought for. After destruction of Vatican City, they will unanimously war against Christ at his coming to establish millennial reign. This is battle of Armageddon.

"These shall make war with the Lamb, and the Lamb shall overcome them: for he is Lord of lords, and King of kings: and they that are with him are called, and chosen, and faithful." Revelation 17 verse 14

The Son of Man Is Given Dominion

"I saw in the night visions, and, behold, one like the Son of man came with the clouds of heaven, and came to the Ancient of days, and they brought him near before him. And there was given him dominion, and glory, and a kingdom, that all people, nations, and languages, should serve him: his dominion is an everlasting dominion, which shall not pass away, and his kingdom that which shall not be destroyed." Daniel 7 verse 13

"And in the days of these kings shall the God of heaven set up a kingdom, which shall never be destroyed: and the kingdom shall not be left to other people, but it shall break in pieces and consume all these kingdoms, and it shall stand for ever. Forasmuch as thou sawest that the stone was cut out of the mountain without hands, and that it brake in pieces the iron, the brass, the clay, the silver, and the gold; the great God hath made known to the king what shall come to pass hereafter: and the dream is certain, and the interpretation thereof sure." Daniel 2 verses 44 to 45

"And I saw heaven opened, and behold a white horse; and he that sat upon him was called Faithful and True, and in righteousness he doth judge and make war. His eyes were as a flame of fire, and on his head were many crowns; and he had a name written, that no man knew, but he himself. And he was clothed with a vesture dipped in blood: and his name is called The Word of God. And the armies which were in heaven followed him upon white horses, clothed in fine linen, white and clean. And out of his mouth goeth a sharp sword, that with it he should smite the nations: and he shall rule them with a rod of iron: and he treadeth the winepress of the fierceness and wrath of Almighty God. And he hath on his vesture and on his thigh a name written, KING OF KINGS, AND LORD OF LORDS. And I saw an angel standing in the sun; and he cried with a loud voice, saying to all the fowls that fly in the midst of heaven, Come and gather yourselves together unto the supper of the great God; hat ye may

eat the flesh of kings, and the flesh of captains, and the flesh of mighty men, and the flesh of horses, and of them that sit on them, and the flesh of all men, both free and bond, both small and great. And I saw the beast, and the kings of the earth, and their armies, gathered together to make war against him that sat on the horse, and against his army. And the beast was taken, and with him the false prophet that wrought miracles before him, with which he deceived them that had received the mark of the beast, and them that worshipped his image. These both were cast alive into a lake of fire burning with brimstone. And the remnant were slain with the sword of him that sat upon the horse, which sword proceeded out of his mouth: and all the fowls were filled with their flesh." Revelation 19 verse 11 to 21

Jesus Christ will overcome them. No flesh will remain on the earth this time. Christ and His saints will establish his millennial reign on the earth. Satan will be imprisoned for one thousand years. He will not be allowed to be moving about the way he is right now.

"And I saw an angel come down from heaven, having the key of the bottomless pit and a great chain in his hand. And he laid hold on the dragon, that old serpent, which is the Devil, and Satan, and bound him a thousand years, And cast him into the bottomless pit, and shut him up, and set a seal upon him, that he should deceive the nations no more, till the thousand years should be fulfilled: and after that he must be loosed a little season." Revelation 20 verses 1 to 3

After Millenium, he will be set loose to convince those that resurrected unto death that God is not just with them.   On the other hand, books of record will be opened, and all the condemned that have been in hell fire will be judged according to what they did when they were in the flesh.

"And I saw thrones, and they sat upon them, and judgment was given unto them: and I saw the souls of them that were beheaded for the witness of Jesus, and for the word of God, and

which had not worshipped the beast, neither his image, neither had received his mark upon their foreheads, or in their hands; and they lived and reigned with Christ a thousand years. But the rest of the dead lived not again until the thousand years were finished. This is the first resurrection." Revelation 20 verses 4 to 5

The saints that were beheaded or killed in various forms because of their faith in Christ during the tribulation, will resurrect to join the saints that were raptured to reign with Christ during the Millenium, this is the first resurrection or resurrection unto life

"Now if Christ be preached that he rose from the dead, how say some among you that there is no resurrection of the dead? But if there be no resurrection of the dead, then is Christ not risen: And if Christ be not risen, then is our preaching vain, and your faith is also vain. Yea, and we are found false witnesses of God; because we have testified of God that he raised up Christ: whom he raised not up, if so be that the dead rise not. For if the dead rise not, then is not Christ raised: And if Christ be not raised, your faith is vain; ye are yet in your sins. Then they also which are fallen asleep in Christ are perished. If in this life only we have hope in Christ, we are of all men most miserable. But now is Christ risen from the dead, and become the firstfruits of them that slept. For since by man came death, by man came also the resurrection of the dead. For as in Adam all die, even so in Christ shall all be made alive. But every man in his own order: Christ the firstfruits; afterward they that are Christ's at his coming. Then cometh the end, when he shall have delivered up the kingdom to God, even the Father; when he shall have put down all rule and all authority and power. For he must reign, till he hath put all enemies under his feet.The last enemy that shall be destroyed is death. For he hath put all things under his feet. But when he saith all things are put under him, it is manifest that he is excepted, which did put all things under him. And when all things shall be subdued unto him, then shall the Son also himself be subject unto him that put all things under him, that God may be all in all. Else what shall they do which are baptized for the dead, if the dead rise not at all? why are they then baptized for the dead? And why stand we in jeopardy every hour? I protest by your rejoicing which I have in Christ Jesus our Lord, I

die daily. If after the manner of men I have fought with beasts at Ephesus, what advantageth it me, if the dead rise not? let us eat and drink; for tomorrow we die. Be not deceived: evil communications corrupt good manners. Awake to righteousness, and sin not; for some have not the knowledge of God: I speak this to your shame.

The Resurrection Body

But some man will say, How are the dead raised up? and with what body do they come? Thou fool, that which thou sowest is not quickened, except it die: And that which thou sowest, thou sowest not that body that shall be, but bare grain, it may chance of wheat, or of some other grain: But God giveth it a body as it hath pleased him, and to every seed his own body. All flesh is not the same flesh: but there is one kind of flesh of men, another flesh of beasts, another of fishes, and another of birds. There are also celestial bodies, and bodies terrestrial: but the glory of the celestial is one, and the glory of the terrestrial is another. There is one glory of the sun, and another glory of the moon, and another glory of the stars: for one star differeth from another star in glory. So also is the resurrection of the dead. It is sown in corruption; it is raised in incorruption: It is sown in dishonour; it is raised in glory: it is sown in weakness; it is raised in power: It is sown a natural body; it is raised a spiritual body. There is a natural body, and there is a spiritual body. And so it is written, The first man Adam was made a living soul; the last Adam was made a quickening spirit. Howbeit that was not first which is spiritual, but that which is natural; and afterward that which is spiritual. The first man is of the earth, earthy: the second man is the Lord from heaven. As is the earthy, such are they also that are earthy: and as is the heavenly, such are they also that are heavenly. And as we have borne the image of the earthy, we shall also bear the image of the heavenly.

Mystery and Victory

Now this I say, brethren, that flesh and blood cannot inherit the kingdom of God; neither doth corruption inherit incorruption. Behold, I shew you a mystery; We shall not all sleep, but we shall all be changed, In a moment, in the twinkling of an eye, at the last trump: for the trumpet shall sound, and the dead shall be raised incorruptible, and we shall be changed. For this corruptible must put on incorruption, and this mortal must put on immortality. So when this corruptible shall have put on incorruption, and this mortal shall have put on immortality, then shall be brought to pass the saying that is written, Death is swallowed up in victory. O death, where is thy sting? O grave, where is thy victory? The sting of death is sin; and the strength of sin is the law. But thanks be to God, which giveth us the victory through our Lord Jesus Christ. Therefore, my beloved brethren, be ye stedfast, unmoveable, always abounding in the work of the Lord, forasmuch as ye know that your labour is not in vain in the Lord." 1st Corinthians 15 verses 12 to 58

After the Millenium, Sinners in hell will resurrect, this is resurrection unto death. They will be judged according to the record of how they rejected Christ and lived according to the dictates of their mind. Thereafter, both them, Lucifer, and hell will be cast into Lake of fire. This is the second death or eternal death.

The New Heaven and New earth will be established, where there is no sin, and no sorrow, with the New Jerusalem as the capital City.

The New Heaven and the New Earth

"And I saw a new heaven and a new earth: for the first heaven and the first earth were passed away; and there was no more sea. And I John saw the holy city, new Jerusalem, coming down from God out of heaven, prepared as a bride adorned for her husband. And I heard a great voice out of heaven saying, Behold, the tabernacle of God is with men, and he will dwell with them, and they shall be his people, and God himself shall be with them, and be their God. And God shall wipe away all tears from their eyes; and there shall be no more death, neither sorrow, nor crying, neither shall there be any more pain: for the former things are passed away. And he that sat upon the throne said, Behold, I make all things new. And he said unto me, Write: for these words are true and faithful. And he said unto me, It is done. I am Alpha and Omega, the beginning and the end. I will give unto him that is athirst of the fountain of the water of life freely. He that overcometh shall inherit all things; and I will be his God, and he shall be my son." Revelation 21 verses 1 to 7

World War III that is now brewing, is a significant pointer to the fact that the end of the world, rapture and second coming of Christ is very near. Make haste to be saved. Very soon nothing will matter anymore on the earth, except what you do with Jesus Christ and His Word. Wealth, fame and beauty will lose meaning and significance.

Be wise. Seek the salvation of Jesus Christ now. Don't let Catholic idolatry deceive you. Run for your life. The time is up.

God Bless you.

My other books which may be of benefit to you are:

Third World War or World War III

My Love

Interplanetary Citizenship

Excelling Wisdom

Battle Cry

Born to Rule

Where Is My Husband?

Steps to Activate Your Authority in Christ

Spiritual Remote Control

Great Contention

Proof of Creation and the Creator

Golden Vessel

Effects of third Party Interest on Marriage.

The Privilege of Predestination

New World Order and the Repercussion

Panacea for Marital Discord.

Simplified Accounting and Finance for Business Growth

Business Accounting

Financial Analysis and Internal Control. - Business Managers' Companion

Vatican City in Prophecy

 The Perfect Bride